craft **workshop**

string

craft **workshop**

string

Deena Beverley

photography by Peter Williams

southwater

This edition is published by Southwater

Southwater is an imprint of Anness Publishing Ltd
Hermes House, 88–89 Blackfriars Road, London SE1 8HA
tel. 020 7401 2077; fax 020 7633 9499
www.southwaterbooks.com; info@anness.com

This edition distributed in the UK by The Manning
Partnership Ltd, 6 The Old Dairy,
Melcombe Road, Bath BA2 3LR;
tel. 01225 478 444; fax 01225 478 440;
sales@manning-partnership.co.uk

This edition distributed in the USA and Canada by National
Book Network, 4720 Boston Way, Lanham, MD 20706;
tel. 301 459 3366; fax 301 459 1705; www.nbnbooks.com

This edition distributed in Australia by Pan Macmillan
Australia, Level 18, St Martins Tower,
31 Market St, Sydney, NSW 2000;
tel. 1300 135 113; fax 1300 135 103;
customer.service@macmillan.com.au

This edition distributed in New Zealand by The Five Mile
Press (NZ) Ltd, PO Box 33–1071 Takapuna, Unit
11/101–111 Diana Drive, Glenfield, Auckland 10;
tel. (09) 444 4144; fax (09) 444 4518;
fivemilenz@clear.net.nz

Previously published as *New Crafts: Stringwork*

PUBLISHER: JOANNA LORENZ
SENIOR EDITOR: CLARE NICHOLSON
PHOTOGRAPHER: PETER WILLIAMS
DESIGNER: CAROLINE REEVES
STYLIST: DEENA BEVERLEY
ILLUSTRATOR: VANA HAGGERTY

10 9 8 7 6 5 4 3 2 1

CONTENTS

INTRODUCTION

THE DECORATIVE USE OF STRING AND ROPE HAS ENJOYED A RENAISSANCE IN RECENT YEARS. WHETHER THEY ARE WRAPPED SIMPLY AROUND RUSTIC-STYLED CANDLE HOLDERS, OR WORKED INTO THE ELABORATE TRIMMINGS KNOWN AS PASSEMENTERIE, THE ONGOING PASSION FOR ALL THINGS NATURAL HAS GIVEN THEM RENEWED PROMINENCE AS FAVOURED MATERIALS OF DESIGNERS AND ARTISTS AROUND THE WORLD.

STRING AND ROPE CAN BE FOUND IN MANY KINDS OF SHOP. AS WELL AS OBVIOUS SOURCES — SUCH AS HIGH-STREET HARDWARE SUPPLIERS AND DEPARTMENT STORES — EVEN THE MOST SEEMINGLY INCONGRUOUS OUTLETS ARE LIKELY TO HAVE A SUPPLY OF SOME TYPE OF ROPE OR STRING. IT IS THIS UNIVERSAL ACCESSIBILITY, AS WELL AS THE LOW COST OF THE RAW MATERIALS, THAT HELPS TO MAKE THEM SUCH APPEALING MEDIA WITH WHICH TO WORK.

Left: The diversity of the colours and textures of string materials allows scope for creating wonderful objects. The balls and spools of string also create a decorative object in their own right.

STRING AND ROPE – A TRADITIONAL CRAFT

FROM SIMPLE, HANDMADE, TWO-STRAND TWISTS TO COMPLEX MACHINE-MADE ROPES BUILT AROUND A STURDY CORE, STRING AND ROPE HAVE BEEN KEPT AND USED IN ALMOST EVERY HOME IN THE WORLD. THEY HAVE BEEN FASHIONED INTO AN AMAZINGLY DIVERSE RANGE OF PRACTICAL AND DECORATIVE ITEMS, INCLUDING BANISTER ROPES IN GRAND HOUSES, THATCH-TYING MATERIALS ON CROFTERS' COTTAGES, AS WELL AS STRAPS, BELTS, SLINGS AND BASKETS IN PRIMITIVE CULTURES.

Ropework is one of the oldest folk arts. Initially seized upon and perfected by sailors, almost every walk of life has borrowed from the art. Anglers, farmers, butchers, cooks, coopers, firemen, florists, gardeners, homemakers, upholsterers, bookbinders, boy and girl scouts, hot-air balloonists and even tree surgeons all produce knots peculiar to their tasks.

As with all folk arts, necessity bred invention, with the available materials determining the crafts that were practised. A multitude of fibres – vegetable, animal and synthetic – have been twisted together to produce strong rope formations in almost every culture. Naval seamen have traditionally specialized in the technique of square knotting (macramé), as only log line, fishing line and other thin materials were available in sufficient quantities for practice work. Merchant sailors were generally better supplied and, although they were seldom issued with new rope, the range of discarded materials that they could use was more varied, resulting in heavier, ornate work known as decorative marlingspike seamanship (applied knots).

The interest of seamen in their knots was widespread, intense and often fiercely competitive. Complex knots were explained under pledge of secrecy, and knowledge of one knot was often bartered for that of another. Superlative knot-makers were very highly regarded. A great many small items were required on board ship; these were produced by the sailors

on board, and included everything from handles for chests, doors, buckets and drawers to fastenings on laundry and ditty bags (small bags that the sailors used to hold needles and thread).

Indeed, one of the earliest volumes devoted to the subject – *The Book of Knots*, published by Hodge and Chamier in 1866 – appeared under the nautical-sounding pseudonym of "Tom Bowling" to impress its sea-loving readers.

Above: String and rope have always been widely used in nautical applications. Sailors traditionally have great skill and knowledge of knots and ropecraft.

The undisputed king of knots is Clifford W. Ashley, although he ascribes an authoritative status to Darcy Lever, author of *Sheet Anchor* (1808). *The Ashley Book of Knots* was truly a life's work, comprising instructions for over 4000 knots.

Above: The wildly contrasting repair on this synthetic net bag emphasizes the workaday nature of nautical knotting. Whatever materials are to hand are used.

Left: Fenders on ships are made in a wide range of knots. They are designed to prevent the paintwork from being scuffed as the ship enters port; similarly elaborate knot formations appear on floats.

Above: Twisted and knotted rope forms a sturdy handle for this urn.

Only knots that were functional in nature were included in Ashley's book, but throughout history decorative knots, which would in reality be impractical, have featured as a motif in art. Such knots appear on tombstones, early book covers, ancient architectural carvings and in illuminated manuscripts. Knots were used in many heraldic devices, and artists such as Leonardo da Vinci have drawn elaborate knot forms in their work. Patterns have also been created by pressing rope into the surface of wet clay to produce an imprint, and by the ever-popular decorative technique of using twisted ropes of china clay to embellish simple pots and fine porcelain alike.

Knotting formed the basis of string and rope crafts from the ninth century onwards, but contemporary work features many other techniques, some utilizing little more than a simple wrapping of string or rope. Christian Astuguevielle has made rope-wrapping into an art form, and the rope-wrapped chair shown in this book is a homage to his work. (The string-wrapped tumblers and the string-wrapped candelabra are less demanding versions of this technique.)

Whether looped loosely around a muslin curtain as a delightfully simple tieback, or worked into fantastically complex knots and tassels for more elaborate tastes, these inexpensive and universally available materials have something to offer everyone.

GALLERY

STRING IS AN EXTREMELY VERSATILE MEDIUM WHICH HAS BEEN USED IN CRAFTWORK FOR MANY YEARS. PRESENTED HERE IS A SELECTION OF THE WIDE RANGE OF OBJECTS THAT CAN BE MADE USING STRING OR ROPE.

ONCE YOU HAVE PRACTISED THE BASIC TECHNIQUES AND WORKED ON SOME OF THE PROJECTS IN THE FOLLOWING PAGES, THESE GALLERY ITEMS WILL PROVIDE FURTHER PRACTICAL AND INSPIRATIONAL IDEAS.

Left: The string bag is a design classic. It is lightweight, can be packed away to nothing when not in use, and allows ventilation of fruit and vegetables when in transit.

Above: Earthy terracotta is offset by smooth, white rope in a practical wine cooler that will withstand years of use.

Left: When making household objects, the method of coiling rope is most often associated with table mats. This dice cup is another use of this simple method, creating an attractive yet functional object.

Above: Some macramé pieces are of such simple design that they are timeless. This child's chair would look adorable hanging from a sturdy tree in the garden.

Right: Cotton string loses its utilitarian image when glamorized with a verdigris paint effect and gilded in metal leaf.

Opposite: Those practising the passementiere's art are constantly finding new and exciting materials which reflect trends in interior design. Smooth metal contrasts beautifully with rough jute in this elegant group of tassels.

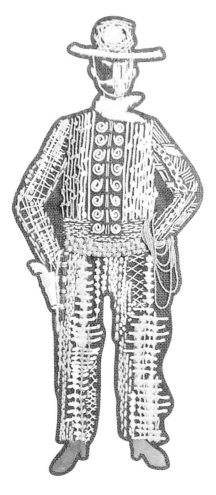

Above: String can also be used as an art material. This cowboy is appliquéd using string to give a wonderful collage effect.

Left: Beauty rests in utility, as this restrained turned wooden string store, holding a satisfyingly large ball of garden twine, proves admirably.

Far left: This wonderfully decorative bell knocker has been elaborately knotted and finished with a Turk's Head knot.

Left: A simple wrapping of green garden twine adds rustic charm to a plain, turned candlestick.

MATERIALS

STRING AND ROPE ARE AVAILABLE IN A WONDERFUL ARRAY OF SIZES, COLOURS AND MATERIALS, BOTH NATURAL AND ARTIFICIAL. THROUGHOUT HISTORY THEY HAVE BEEN MADE FROM WHATEVER HAS COME TO HAND, INCLUDING NETTLES, HEMP AND BLACKBERRY STALKS.

MANY OF THE PROJECTS IN THIS BOOK USE UNUSUAL MATERIALS THAT GIVE STRIKING RESULTS, SUCH AS RAFFIA, PAPER ROPE AND BUILDER'S BRICK LINE. CHOOSE ACCORDING TO THE EFFECT YOU WISH TO ACHIEVE: SMOOTH FOR AN ELEGANT FINISH, OR TEXTURED FOR RUSTIC APPEAL.

Plasterer's jute scrim is an open woven mesh used to make joints. The plaster is forced through the holes to adhere smoothly, creating a firm bond. In string crafts, scrim is a decorative material forming attractive fringes and netting.

Polyester rope is suitable for heavy-duty use, as it is very strong. Available in a variety of thicknesses and colours, it will give a contemporary, urban feel to many of the projects in this book. For instance, by substituting a vivid polyester rope for the natural sash cord used for the deckchair, and painting the wooden frame a bright colour, an entirely different look could be achieved. Polyester rope is available from hardware stores, as well as from outlets stocking ship chandlery and climbing equipment.

Sisal rope and string are made from the prepared fibre of the agave and fourcroya plants. They are very strong and pleasingly textural.

Coir rope is made from coconut husks. It is strong and, as you would expect, hairy. It is perfect for projects in which a naive, "rough-and-ready" finish is required.

Sash cord is available in both waxed and unwaxed forms from hardware stores. It is made in different materials, including jute and polypropylene, and in several colours, including white, natural and white with red flecks. Sash cord is strong enough to bear the weight of heavy windows, and it is ideal for applications requiring a durable finish, such as the deckchair. The wide bore of this cord makes it quick to work,

and it produces a chunky, substantial-looking finish.

Piping cord, widely available from department stores and haberdashers, is firm and flexible. It comes in several different thicknesses.

Cotton rope is soft, malleable and wonderfully easy to work with, yet gives a durable, strong finish. It holds three-dimensional shapes well, such as in the Woven Stool Seat project. It is available from hardware shops.

Cotton string is flexible and of delicate colouring, making it perfect for projects requiring a subtle, tensile quality, such as the String-trimmed Bag.

Flax rope, made from flax fibre, is incredibly durable. Pieces of flax linen have been found in the pyramids of Egypt in remarkably sound condition.

Paper cord has become tremendously popular in floristry and gift-wrapping in

recent years. Some varieties unravel to produce a wide ribbon that holds three-dimensional shapes well; whilst others are designed to be used purely as strong, decorative cord.

Jute string is made in both tarred and untarred forms. Tar gives a rich, dark sheen to the twine and renders it more weatherproof, so this type is perfect for garden applications; untarred string is better suited to most indoor craft projects. Both types of jute string are available from hardware and garden-supply stores.

Raffia is ideal for gift-wrapping and floristry work, and it is available from garden-supply stores, stationers and in bulk from specialist craft suppliers.

Garden twine is also available from hardware and garden-supply stores. It comes in many shades of green, as well as in its natural colour.

KEY

1 Plasterer's jute scrim	12 Flax rope
2 Polyester rope	13 Piping cord
3 Sisal	14 Paper cord
4 Sisal	15 Jute string
5 Coir rope	16 White cotton string
6 Red-flecked sash cord	17 Raffia
7 Sash cord	18 Green garden twine
8 Sash cord	19 Green garden twine
9 Piping cord	20 Brown garden twine
10 Cotton rope	
11 Cotton string	

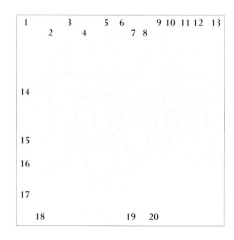

EQUIPMENT

ONLY THE MOST BASIC TOOLS AND EQUIPMENT ARE REQUIRED TO PRODUCE ALL THE PROJECTS IN THIS BOOK, ALTHOUGH MORE SPECIALIZED EQUIPMENT — SUCH AS A ROTARY HOLE PUNCH AND A GLUE GUN — WILL MAKE LARGER-SCALE PROJECTS EASIER AND MORE PLEASANT TO WORK.

CHOOSING AND USING THE CORRECT EQUIPMENT WILL ENSURE NEAT AND PROFESSIONAL RESULTS. THE SINGLE MOST IMPORTANT TOOL IS, OF COURSE, YOUR HANDS: INDEED, MOST STRING- AND ROPEWORK HAS BEEN PRACTISED FOR CENTURIES USING NO ADDITIONAL EQUIPMENT WHATSOEVER.

High-tack PVA glue is an absolute dream for use in string crafts. It allows bonding of string, even to difficult vertical surfaces, with pinpoint accuracy, cleanliness and economy.

Instant bonding (cyano-acrylate) glue is superb for dripping on to string to prevent ends from unravelling.

Spray adhesive is useful for delicate work that would be disturbed by a brush application of glue, although any "over-spray" can be messy and difficult to clean up. Only use when it is not possible to glue by other methods.

Glue gun and glue sticks are ideal for heavy-duty applications, particularly those requiring adhesion to vertical or curved surfaces. An instant bond is easily formed, although excess strands of glue can be tedious to remove. Be careful not to burn your hands on the hot glue.

Adhesive applicators Wooden tongue depressors and wooden skewers are perfect for applying glue.

Measuring equipment Accuracy in measuring will ensure professional results. A soft pencil, set square and metal ruler are all essential tools.

Cutting equipment A craft knife, scalpel and scissors will be sufficient to make all the projects in this book. For safety and accuracy, always use a clean, sharp blade in the knife and scalpel. A cutting mat, while not essential, will protect your work surface, aid accuracy and preserve the life of a blade. Alternatively, work on a pile of magazines.

Painting equipment In addition to a range of paintbrushes, a small sponge roller (used with a paint tray) will be useful for string painting, and some wood offcuts will make handy stamping blocks. Emulsion, acrylic and gouache paints have been used for projects throughout. Choose paint that is right for the job, for example, fast-drying stamping paint (available from stationers and art supply shops) will make the gift-wrap project clean and quick to do. A paint palette is useful if you are working with small quantities of several different colours. Always have a jar of water to clean your brush in if you are using water-based paints. If you are painting with oils, clean the brushes in white spirit immediately after use.

Wood filler with a spatula for mixing and a palette knife for easy application, can be used to fill gaps and to smooth surfaces. The surface can then be further smoothed with wire wool or a sanding block once dry.

Fabric stiffener is easy to apply, and it gives fabric and string additional body stiffness. It is also used when covering moulds, as in the Food Cover.

Hammer and awl A hammer and awl are useful for driving rope securely into place when it has been so tightly woven that it becomes taut and difficult to work.

Rotary hole punch This is useful as a tool for making holes of various sizes, and it will add a smooth, professional finish to many of the projects in this book.

Cordless drill/screwdriver If you are planning to work on several projects, a cordless drill or screwdriver will be a sound investment. Choose a drill or screwdriver that can also be used manually.

Needles and bodkins For thicker cords the glue-dripping method will not provide a sufficiently fine point to the string for it to be threaded through a needle so a bodkin, which is a curved needle with a larger eye, will be required. A sewing needle is also needed for some of the basic stitching involved. Choose the correct-sized eye for the width of the string or thread.

Beads will add glamour and textural interest to string and rope projects. Choose carefully for a sophisticated, understated result.

Pegs and clips Clothes pegs and metal clips are very useful for holding string or rope in place as it dries, particularly on more challenging wrapping projects such as the chair. Although the adhesives recommended throughout will form fast, secure bonds, clamping a piece of work in place as the glue sets will ensure ease of working and consistent, neat results. Clothes pegs are also helpful for holding string in position at a safe distance from your fingers as instant-bonding glue is dripped on to it for ease of threading.

Release agents When shaping string or rope around a mould, as in the Food Cover, use of the appropriate release agents (clear plastic wrap and petroleum jelly, in this case) will ensure that you can

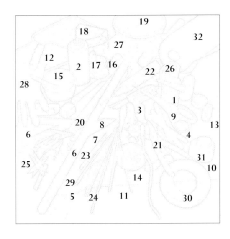

release the finished item smoothly from the mould.

Protective and clean-up equipment
When working with adhesives and paint, it is wise to protect your work surface from drips and splashes before you begin. Brown paper is better for this purpose than newspaper, as newsprint could transfer itself on to pale string or delicate papers. Masking tape can be used to cover specific areas before painting or using adhesive; the low-tack variety is ideal. Absorbent kitchen paper will be useful to mop up any spills. Protect your hands with disposable plastic gloves when working with adhesive.

KEY
1 High-tack PVA glue
2 Spray adhesive
3 Glue gun and glue sticks
4 Tongue depressors and wooden skewers
5 Soft pencil
6 Metal ruler and set square
7 Scalpel
8 Craft knife
9 Scissors
10 Cutting mat
11 Paintbrushes
12 Small sponge roller and paint tray
13 Fast-drying stamp paints
14 Paint palette
15 Wood filler, with spatula
16 Palette knife
17 Wire wool
18 Sanding block
19 Fabric stiffener
20 Hammer
21 Rotary hole punch
22 Cordless drill/screwdriver and attachments
23 Needles
24 Large bodkins
25 Clothes pegs and metal clips
26 Petroleum jelly
27 Clear plastic wrap
28 Disposable plastic gloves
29 Brown paper and other papers
30 Masking tape
31 Water
32 Absorbent kitchen paper

BASIC TECHNIQUES

STRING AND ROPE ARE AMAZINGLY VERSATILE MEDIA — THEY MAY BE PLAITED, COILED, WOVEN, WRAPPED, KNOTTED, APPLIQUÉD, EMBROIDERED AND EVEN KNITTED INTO SIMPLE OR COMPLEX PATTERNS FOR PRACTICAL OR DECORATIVE PURPOSES. IT IS QUITE MAGICAL THAT WITH JUST A FEW BASIC TECHNIQUES AN ESSENTIALLY ONE-DIMENSIONAL MATERIAL CAN ASSUME ALMOST ANY FORM.

The enthusiastic stringworker can learn complex knots and embark upon fine embroidery and passementerie projects, but even a young child can tackle stringwork. Cat's cradle is a simple and popular game that introduces many children to the adaptability of string, not to mention skipping ropes and tug-of-war. Simple knots and whipping are used by almost everyone in every walk of life, for decorative and practical purposes alike. Studying and practising the techniques on these will make the projects in this book even easier.

ESTIMATING YARN REQUIREMENTS

To establish how much string or rope is needed to complete a macramé project, multiply the required finished length by eight then multiply this figure by half the number of strands to be used. This is a sum that sounds far more complex in theory than it is in practice.

THREADING STRING AND ROPE

Threading string and rope through holes and eyelets is a practical way of fastening, as in many nautical uses, but can also be purely decorative, as on the simple lampshade edging illustrated here, or to make an elegant hanging out of found objects.

It is possible to thread string on to a large needle, but this is not always necessary unless you actually plan to stitch with the string as if it were thread.

The raw end of the string or rope can be rendered much more rigid and less likely to fray, and correspondingly easier to thread, if it is treated with fast-drying glue before use.

Preparing the string or rope

1 Catch the end of the string or rope in a wooden clothes peg. Wood is preferable to plastic, as it grips string and rope better, but is not essential.

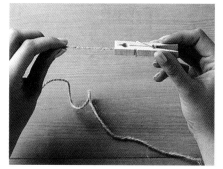

2 Holding the string or rope between the finger and thumb of one hand, rotate the peg until the string or rope becomes tightly twisted but has not quite started to double back on itself.

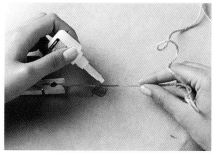

3 Working over a protected surface, drip a few drops of instant-bonding glue on to the string, allowing it to saturate the short length that is held taut between finger and thumb and peg.

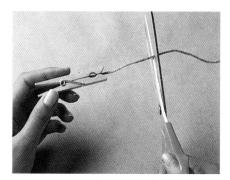

4 Allow the glue to dry thoroughly before snipping halfway through the glued part of the string or rope. The end is now narrow and firm enough to thread comfortably. This gluing technique can be used to seal the other end of the string or rope when the project is complete.

Whatever the project, make sure the hole through which the string or rope will be threaded is an appropriate size. This may sound like stating the obvious, but if the hole is too small, an uneven, strained look will result; if the hole is too large (for example if a hole punch with only one, large setting is used), the finish will be ungainly and not at all elegant.

Threading

1 Having taken care to match the width of the string to the size of the hole, pull the string through gently so as not to fray it unduly against the possibly rough interior edges of the punched hole. Brace your other hand against the material through which you are threading so that it does not become creased or distorted as the string is passed through it.

2 When most of the string has passed through the hole, take care to consider exactly how tightly it needs to be threaded for the best decorative effect. A gentle tension, leaving loops of even size, adds sophistication to this lampshade.

APPLIQUÉ WITH STRING AND ROPE

All manner of delightful designs can be wrought by stitching simple swirls of string or rope on to fabrics. Choose a string or rope to complement or contrast with the base fabric. Here a soft, pure wool blanket with a floppy fringe gains tough chic appliquéd with a single strand pulled from a three-strand sisal rope packed with rough-and-ready texture.

1 Allow the string or rope to untwist on to the surface of the fabric. As you allow it to uncoil, it will naturally fall into twists and swirls, which it is difficult and unnecessary to improve upon.

2 If you are a beginner, you may like to safety pin the design in place before stitching. Ease the swirls into position without affecting the actual pattern, so that the design is evenly spaced from the edge of the fabric.

3 Thread a needle with strong toning thread. Secure the thread in place on the surface of the fabric with a few stitches in a place that will be hidden when the string or rope has been appliquéd. Pick up a tiny piece of the fabric with the needle along the line where the string or rope will lie.

4 Bring the needle up through the string or rope. Pull the thread taut.

5 Take the needle back through the string or rope, concealing the thread within its twists and working along the design. Continue to slip stitch the design in this way.

WHIPPING

This is a technique of binding together one or more lengths of rope using either twine or string. When finished, the ends are invisible and the finish is very strong and neat.

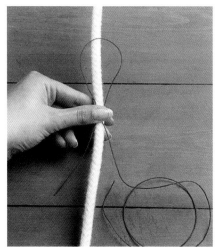

1 Take the end of a length of twine and form a loop leaving about 8cm (3in) at one end. Position the loop against the string or rope where the binding is to begin.

2 Wrap the other end of the twine round both the rope and twine several times, working towards the loop.

3 Keep the twine bound closely together and work with an even tension. Do not bind over the top of the loop. When the section of binding is long enough, pass the end of the twine that you have been working with through the loop.

4 With one hand, pull the other end of the twine, making the loop smaller and smaller, until it pulls the end of the twine that you were binding with down under the binding. Trim the ends.

KNOTS AND STITCHES
Crown Sennit

This type of knot can be made from between three and six lengths of string. Once formed, a knot, or "crown", can be linked to another and so on to build up a "sennit". This continuous knotted length is strong and can be used for a range of purposes. Successive crowns may be made in alternate directions (anti-clockwise and then clockwise), if desired, to produce a spiral effect. The success of the sennit depends on drawing up the crowns evenly.

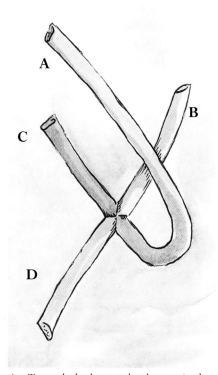

1 To work the knot, take the required number of strings (in this case, four) and whip them together in the centre, as shown. Cross string A over string B.

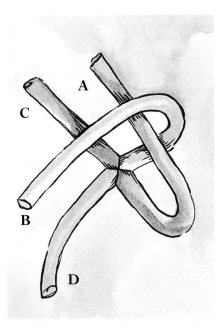

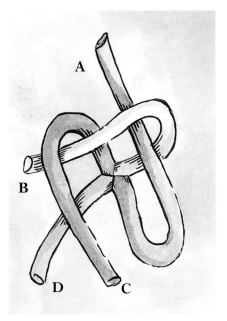

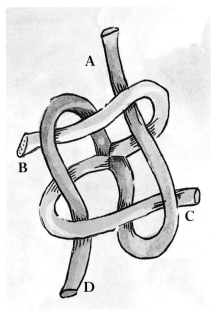

2 Then, cross string B over strings A and C.

3 Next, cross string C over strings B and D.

4 Pass string D over string C and then down through the loop that was formed with string A. Tighten each string gradually to make an even knot. Repeat the process to create the next knot.

Lark's Head Knot

This useful knot, known as a "mounting knot", is often used to mount strings on to a base string, called a "knot anchor", in macramé projects. Any length of string can be used to make the knot, but it must be long enough to pass through the loop.

1 Fold the string in half to make a loop. Hold the loop in front of the "anchor", bend the loop down behind it and then thread through the ends from front to back. Pull the ends to secure the knot.

Flat Knot

This basic knot (also known as a "square knot") is usually worked on a group of four strings that have been knotted on to a "knot anchor" using lark's head knots. Only the outer strings are used to create the knot, so that the inner strings become "knot bearers". Successive knots can be worked in this way to create a neat, strong cord.

1 Attach two looped strings side by side on the "knot anchor" using lark's head knots. Take the right-hand string over the two centre strings and then under the left-hand string.

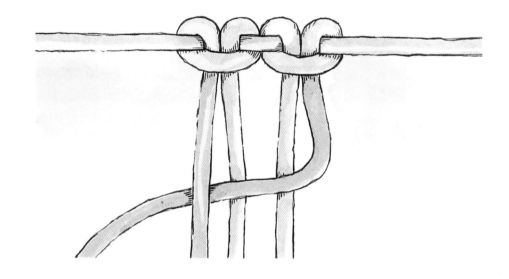

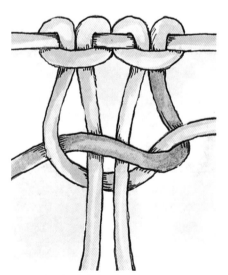

2 Take the left-hand string over the end of this right-hand string, then behind the two centre strings and up over the right-hand string.

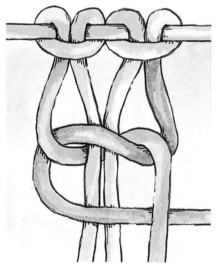

3 Repeat step 1, working from left to right with the right-hand string.

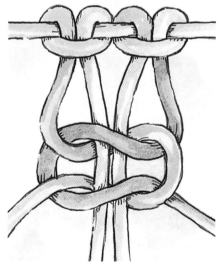

4 Repeat step 2, working from right to left with the left-hand string. Draw up the ends evenly to secure the knot.

Feather Stitch

This attractive looped stitch is very quick and easy to work, but the stitches must be made evenly to create a neat, regular effect. The stitches are worked on either side of an imaginary central line, and they alternate on either side as the row progresses.

Blanket stitch

This straightforward stitch is most commonly used to finish edges in order to prevent fraying or unravelling, especially on blankets (hence the name). The stitches should be spaced at even intervals, although the "arms" of the stitches can be worked at varying lengths for a decorative finish. Blanket stitch can also be used as a form of decorative knotwork.

1 Make the knot in the string, then bring the bodkin up through from the wrong side of the fabric at A. Insert the bodkin at B and bring it out again at C, passing the string beneath the point of the bodkin before drawing it through. Repeat at even intervals.

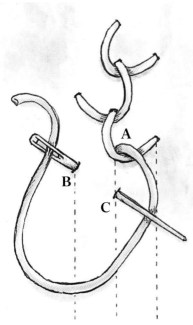

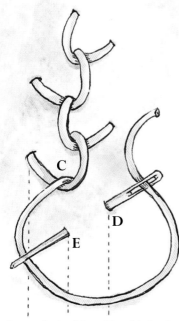

1 Make a knot in the string, then bring the bodkin up through from the wrong side of the fabric at A. Insert it at B and bring it out again at C, passing the string beneath the point of the bodkin before drawing it through.

2 Insert the bodkin at D and bring it out again at E, again passing the string beneath the point of the bodkin before drawing it through.

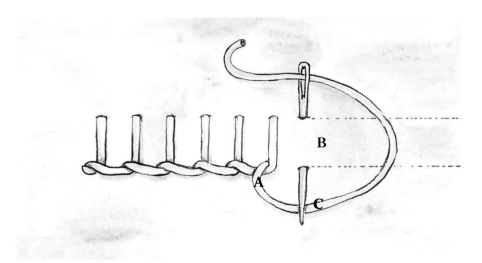

WRAPPED TUMBLERS

THE SIMPLEST APPROACH OFTEN PRODUCES THE MOST PLEASING RESULTS. A BASIC WRAPPING TECHNIQUE IS USED TO COVER THESE TUMBLERS, BUT IT CAN BE DRAMATICALLY VARIED BY USING DIFFERENT WEIGHTS OF STRING. BUILDER'S BRICK LINE PRODUCES A SPARE, ELEGANT FINISH, IN CONTRAST TO THE ROUGH-AND-READY APPEAL OF COIR. THE RELEASE TECHNIQUE USED TO WRAP THE GLASSES MAKES THEM PRACTICAL AS WELL AS STYLISH. THE WRAPPING FITS SNUGLY AND IS SECURE AND COMFORTABLE TO HOLD, YET THE GLASS IS EASILY REMOVED FOR WASHING.

1 Turn each tumbler upside down. If it has a dimple in the base or any other shaping that would make release of the finished wrapping difficult, pad out the hollows with clear plastic wrap and thin card. Wrap the entire tumbler in clear plastic wrap.

2 Decide how far up the glass you want to wrap and, using kitchen paper, cover this area of the plastic wrap with a generous smear of petroleum jelly.

3 Wrap the tumbler in a second layer of clear plastic wrap to cover the petroleum jelly. Tuck the excess plastic wrap inside the tumbler to hold it in place.

4 Starting in the centre of the base, apply high-tack glue to a small area and wind the string in a spiral. Gradually apply more glue as the spiral grows.

5 Continue gluing and wrapping over the edges of the base and up the sides of the tumbler until the desired height is reached.

6 Leave to dry overnight. Gently twist the tumbler to release the bond between the tumbler and the plastic wrap. Remove the tumbler and peel the remaining plastic wrap from the string wrapping. Cut off the excess string using a scalpel. Apply a coat of matt acrylic varnish to seal and protect the wrapping if required.

MATERIALS AND EQUIPMENT YOU WILL NEED

GLASS TUMBLERS • CLEAR PLASTIC WRAP • THIN CARD (OPTIONAL) • KITCHEN PAPER • PETROLEUM JELLY • HIGH-TACK PVA GLUE • GLUE SPREADER • BUILDER'S BRICK LINE, COIR OR SISAL • SCALPEL • MATT ACRYLIC VARNISH (OPTIONAL) • VARNISH BRUSH (OPTIONAL)

STRING-TRIMMED BAG

CAREFULLY APPLIQUÉD ON TO A PLAIN LINEN BAG, PERFECT FOR SHOES OR AS A WASH BAG, COTTON STRING TAKES ON A DELICATE AIR. THE BAG COULD ALSO BE APPLIQUÉD WITH A NAME TO MAKE A PRETTY AND PRACTICAL GIFT. THE COILED ENDS OF THE DRAWSTRING ARE BOTH DECORATIVE AND FUNCTIONAL, PREVENTING THE STRING FROM DISAPPEARING INTO THE CASING WHEN THE BAG IS OPENED.

1 Draw around a small, round object on to paper to make templates for the dots and cut them out. The thickness of the string or piping cord will determine the size of the dots. Fold the fabric in half and arrange the templates on one of the fabric rectangles. Pin in place. Avoid placing them too close to the edges.

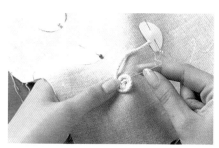

2 Remove one of the templates and mark its position. Pin the end of a length of string or cord on to the centre of the dot. Stitch in place, coiling round and tucking the raw end under as you work.

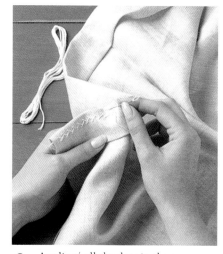

3 Appliqué all the dots in the same way, then fold under the top edge of each rectangle by 1 cm (¹/₂ in). Fold over again a further 4 cm (1¹/₂ in) to make a cuff. Press to mark a guideline. Embroider a row of feather stitch just below the second fold (see Basic Techniques), using three strands of embroidery thread. Unfold the cuff then pin, tack and machine stitch around the two raw edges of the linen. Leave a small gap near the cuff on one side to allow the drawstring to be inserted.

4 Fold down the cuff. Pin, tack and stitch to form a narrow casing at the bottom of the cuff.

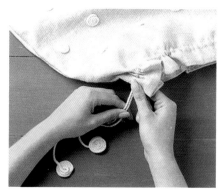

5 Thread string or cord through the casing using a safety pin. Remove the safety pin. Coil each end of the drawstring into a spiral and stitch to secure.

MATERIALS AND EQUIPMENT YOU WILL NEED

PENCIL • SMALL ROUND OBJECT • PAPER • SCISSORS • SOFT WHITE COTTON STRING OR PIPING CORD • 1 PIECE OF NATURAL-COLOURED LINEN FABRIC, 65 X 54 CM (26 X 21¼ IN) • DRESSMAKER'S PINS • SEWING NEEDLE • MATCHING SEWING THREAD • IRON • EMBROIDERY NEEDLE • ECRU STRANDED EMBROIDERY THREAD • TACKING THREAD • SEWING MACHINE • SAFETY PIN

CLASSIC LAMPSHADES

SIMPLE, CLASSIC SHAPES ARE A TIMELESSLY ELEGANT CHOICE FOR LAMPSHADES AND BASES. HOWEVER, CLASSIC NEED NOT MEAN DULL. THE LARGER, CONICAL SHADE IS PRODUCED VERY QUICKLY, USING THE OLD SHADE AS A TEMPLATE; IT IS DECORATED WITH SOFT COTTON STRING CURLICUES, WHICH ADD A DELICATE FLOURISH. THE SMALLER SHADE IS A SHOP-BOUGHT LAMPSHADE PUNCHED WITH HOLES AND THREADED WITH JUTE TWINE. DECORATIVE PENDANTS OF STRING-WRAPPED BEADS OR MARBLES PROVIDE A WITTY NOTE.

1 For the larger shade, first remove the old lampshade from its frame and flatten out. Place it on top of the lampshade stiffener and draw around the outline with a soft pencil.

2 Cut out the shape with scissors or a craft knife.

3 Turn the shape the other way up. Using a scalpel and a metal ruler, cut a line through the protective film on the lampshade stiffener 1 cm ($^1/_2$ in) in from one straight edge. Place the watercolour paper on top of the lampshade stiffener. Ease the protective film away from the stiffener, pulling it with a gentle horizontal, rather than diagonal, motion. Smooth the watercolour paper into position with the flat of your hand.

4 Leave the protective film in place on the 1 cm ($^1/_2$ in) narrow strip that you cut earlier, and finish smoothing the watercolour paper over the lampshade stiffener. Use your thumb to smooth out the paper as you approach the corner.

MATERIALS AND EQUIPMENT YOU WILL NEED

OLD LAMPSHADE • LAMPSHADE STIFFENER • SOFT PENCIL • SCISSORS OR CRAFT KNIFE • SCALPEL • METAL RULER • JAPANESE WATERCOLOUR PAPER • SPRAY ADHESIVE • SOFT WHITE COTTON STRING • JUTE TWINE • CLOTHES PEGS • INSTANT-BONDING GLUE • SHOP-BOUGHT LAMPSHADE • HOLE PUNCH • THREE LARGE BEADS OR MARBLES • COCKTAIL STICKS • HIGH-TACK PVA GLUE

5 Cut away the excess paper. Use a scalpel and metal ruler to cut the paper along the edge of the narrow strip. Remove the protective film from this strip, form the stiffener into a cone shape and overlap the edges. Press the edges firmly together.

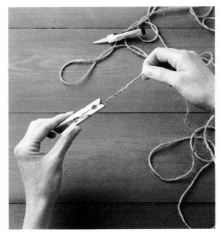

7 For the smaller lampshade, hold one end of the jute twine in a clothes peg and twist tightly. Drip instant-bonding glue on to this end to make a neat end for threading. Allow the glue to dry before snipping off the string close to the peg.

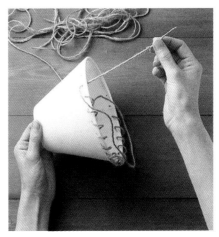

9 Starting at the seam of the lampshade, thread the twine through the holes from front to back. Make sure that the tension is relaxed and even.

6 Spray adhesive on to one side of a generous length of string. Allow the string to fall in a swirling pattern on to the lampshade and press gently into place.

8 Using another clothes peg as a marker to maintain even spacing, make holes around the base of the shop-bought lampshade with a hole punch.

10 When the threading is complete, cut the string and join the two loose ends together using instant-bonding glue.

▶

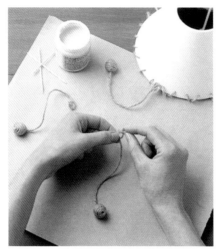

11 To cover the beads or marbles, cut a generous length of twine and fold it in half to find the centre. Using a cocktail stick, apply high-tack PVA glue around the centre of each bead or marble and begin wrapping towards one end, applying more glue as it is needed. Then wrap the other half of the bead or marble in the same way. Cut off one end of twine and leave the other long.

12 Tie a loose, simple knot in the long end of the string and glue it on to the lampshade. Make the other two pendants the same way.

GILDED STRING VASE

The use of gold leaf adds a note of glamour and opulence to create this wonderfully baroque vase. The rough, three-dimensional jute twine and the sheen of the gold leaf contrast very effectively with the smooth, clear glass. Gold leaf and metal leaf are available from good art suppliers or by mail order from specialist suppliers.

1 Wash and dry the vase thoroughly. Draw a wavy line around the top with a chinagraph pencil. Apply glue to one side of the jute twine, blotting off any excess with your finger. Carefully glue the string on to the wavy line, holding each small section in place as it dries. Cut off the string so that the two ends meet exactly. Leave to dry.

2 Glue and stick another piece of string beside the first. Glue two straight lines of string above and below the wavy line. Repeat for the base of the vase.

3 Measure the distance between the string borders and mark on paper. Draw a scroll shape between the two marks, leaving a gap of 1 cm (⅜ in) at each end. Tape the paper inside the vase. Lightly draw over the scroll on to the glass. Remove the template.

4 Glue string on to the scroll. Glue a second piece of string beside the first. Repeat on the opposite side of the vase, then add two more scrolls. Draw wavy lines between the scrolls and cover with string.

5 When the glue is completely dry, paint gilding size on to the string and leave for 10–15 minutes, until tacky. Tear small pieces of gold or metal leaf and place on the string. Press down firmly then gently brush with a fine, dry paintbrush. Gild a small area at a time.

6 Gently brush off some of the gold or metal leaf with a wire brush to produce a distressed look. Rub over the gilded string with a clean fingertip to smooth it out. Clean any excess glue from the vase with a damp cloth or scrape it off with a craft knife.

MATERIALS AND EQUIPMENT YOU WILL NEED

VASE • CHINAGRAPH PENCIL • HIGH-TACK PVA GLUE • JUTE TWINE • SCISSORS • RULER • PAPER • PENCIL • MASKING TAPE • GILDING SIZE •
GOLD LEAF OR DUTCH METAL LEAF • PAINTBRUSH • WIRE BRUSH • CLOTH OR CRAFT KNIFE

PAINTING AND STAMPING WITH STRING

STRING OFFERS MANY EXCITING POSSIBILITIES AS A PAINTING TOOL. COILED AND GLUED ON TO A BLOCK, IT BECOMES A STAMP THAT MAY BE USED TO ANY SCALE. A TINY STRING SPIRAL DIPPED IN PAINT TURNS PLAIN BROWN PAPER INTO PRETTY GIFT-WRAP AND ADDS GLAMOUR TO A HUMBLE PLANT POT. A LARGE COIL OF ROPE PROVIDES AN EXCITING MOTIF FOR DECORATING A PLAIN WALL. WRAPPED AROUND A PAINT ROLLER, STRING PRODUCES RANDOM, WAVY LINES ON GIFT-WRAP THAT ARE REFLECTED IN THE PAPER STRING USED TO TIE THE PARCELS.

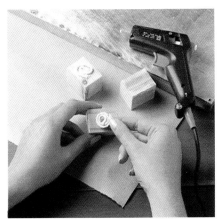

1 To make your own stamps, use a glue gun to stick small spirals of string on to small pieces of wood to make stamping blocks. Leave the glue to set. When gluing small areas, be careful not to burn your fingers on the glue.

2 Thread the plant pot on to a length of sash cord to make the pot easier to paint. Apply a base coat of emulsion or acrylic paint.

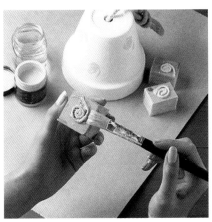

3 When the base coat is dry, apply stamping paint on to one of the spiral stamps using a flat brush. ▶

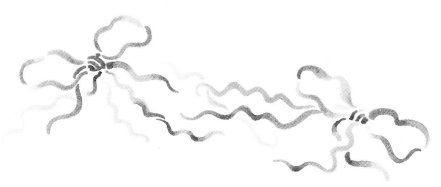

MATERIALS AND EQUIPMENT YOU WILL NEED
GLUE GUN AND GLUE STICKS • WHITE COTTON STRING • SMALL OFFCUTS OF WOOD • PLANT POT • SHORT LENGTH OF SASH CORD • EMULSION OR ACRYLIC PAINT • FAST-DRYING STAMPING PAINT • FLAT PAINTBRUSHES • KITCHEN PAPER • PAINT ROLLER AND TRAY • CRAFT KNIFE • CARDBOARD TUBE • BROWN PARCEL-WRAP

4 Stamp a few times on to kitchen paper to remove the excess paint, then stamp on to the plant pot. If you are stamping with different-coloured paints, use a different stamp for each colour. Leave to dry.

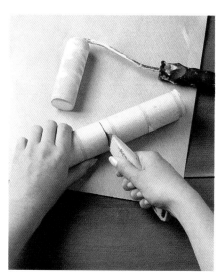

5 To cover a larger area, a paint roller is ideal. Using a craft knife, cut the cardboard tube to fit the paint roller.

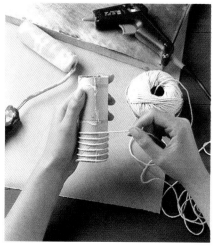

6 Using the glue gun, attach one end of a length of string to the cardboard tube. Wrap the string around the tube in an open spiral. Cut off the string and glue the loose end inside the tube.

7 Slip the cardboard tube over the paint roller, and glue it in place.

8 Pour some emulsion or acrylic paint into the paint tray and run the roller through it. Remove the excess paint by rolling on to kitchen paper.

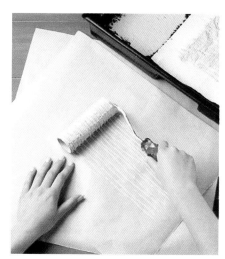

9 Roll the design on to the brown parcel-wrap, pushing the roller with a smooth, consistent action. Leave to dry.

CORD-TRIMMED CUSHION COVERS

SET OFF SIMPLE, EVERYDAY FABRICS WITH WHITE COTTON PIPING CORD AND BRASS EYELETS FOR AN ELEGANTLY MODERN LOOK. THE PLAIN COTTON CUSHION HAS A LOOPED CORD EDGING AND IS FINISHED WITH A DECORATIVE TASSEL AT EACH CORNER. THE CHECK CUSHION, MADE OUT OF A HUMBLE TEA TOWEL, HAS CORD LACED ACROSS THE BACK AND STURDY KNOTS AT THE CORNERS.

1 Using a ruler and felt-tipped pen, draw a 55 cm (21½ in) square and a rectangle 55 x 35 cm (21½ x 14 in) on to the squared pattern paper. Cut out both shapes and pin on to the cotton fabric. Cut one square and two rectangles.

2 Place the square of fabric right side down on a flat surface. Using the dressmaker's pencil, draw a line around the square 3.25 cm (1¼ in) in from the edge. Make marks at 8 cm (3 in) intervals along each line, starting in each corner. Using the eyelet punch and hammer, punch a hole through the fabric at each mark. Position the eyelet pieces either side of the holes and hit firmly with the hammer.

3 Fold in 1 cm (³⁄₈ in) along one long edge of each rectangular piece of fabric. Fold in a further 1.5 cm (½ in) and press. Pin, tack and stitch the hems. Mark a line on the wrong side of the fabric around the three raw edges, 3.25 cm (1¼ in) in from the edge. Make marks at 8 cm (3 in) intervals along each line, starting in each corner. Punch holes in the fabric as before and hammer the eyelets in place.

▶

MATERIALS AND EQUIPMENT YOU WILL NEED

RULER • FELT-TIPPED PEN • SQUARED PATTERN PAPER • SCISSORS • DRESSMAKER'S PINS • COTTON FABRIC • DRESSMAKER'S PENCIL • TAPE MEASURE • EYELET PUNCH • HAMMER • BRASS EYELETS • IRON • SEWING NEEDLE • TACKING THREAD • MATCHING THREAD • SEWING MACHINE • CARD • WHITE COTTON PIPING CORD • FINE WHITE COTTON STRING • 4 BEADS • 2 CUSHION PADS • CHECKED TEA TOWEL

4 Lay the square piece of fabric face up. Place a rectangular piece over it, right sides together, lining up the raw edges. Do the same with the second rectangular piece, so that the two hemmed edges overlap. Pin, tack and stitch a seam all the way around. Clip the corners, turn the cushion right side out and press.

6 Insert a cushion pad. Cut a piece of cord approximately five times the width of the cushion and thread it through the eyelets. Tie the two ends neatly together at the back of the cushion.

8 Mark the positions of the eyelets with the dressmaker's pencil. Punch holes with the eyelet punch through the two layers of fabric along each fold. Hammer the eyelets in place.

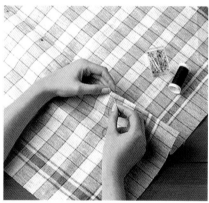

5 Cut two pieces of card 9 x 12 cm (3 1/2 x 4 3/4 in) and place one on top of the other. Wrap the piping cord seven times around the 9 cm (3 1/2 in) depth of the card, starting and ending at one edge.

Thread a piece of fine string between the cards, pull it up to the top and tie in a secure knot. Cut through the piping cord at the opposite end. Unravel the cord and put a bead inside the tassel beneath the knot at the top. Arrange the frayed cord to completely conceal the bead. Bring the two ends of string from the tie down among the frayed cords.

Wrap another piece of string four times around the tassel and tie in a secure knot. Trim the ends of the tassel. Make three more tassels and hand stitch one to each corner of the cushion cover.

7 Cut two more rectangles of cotton fabric using the paper pattern piece cut in Step 1. Trim the tea towel to measure 55 x 70 cm (21 1/2 x 27 1/2 in). Mark a centre line across the shorter width of the tea towel with pins. Make a fold 7.5 cm (3 in) from the centre line on either side, with each fold facing the centre. Press, then tack along each fold 1 cm (1/2 in) from the edge.

9 Hem one edge of the two rectangular pieces as before. Position them on the tea towel piece and pin, tack and stitch together. Clip the corners, turn right side out and press. Mark the position for an eyelet in each corner. Punch holes and hammer the eyelets in place. Insert a cushion pad. Knot a short piece of cord through the eyelet in each corner and knot the ends of the cord to finish. Lace piping cord through the eyelets across the centre of the cover as shown.

TWINE-DECORATED FURNITURE

TRANSFORM A DULL OR SHABBY PIECE OF FURNITURE BY MAKING IT SPROUT GREEN LEAVES! THE LEAVES ARE, APPROPRIATELY ENOUGH, MADE FROM GARDEN TWINE, USING TWO SHADES OF GREEN FOR A THREE-DIMENSIONAL LOOK. THE SURFACE IS TREATED FIRST WITH GREEN WOOD DYE, WHICH HAS THE ADDED ADVANTAGE OF DISGUISING SCRATCHES OR WEAR AND TEAR. TRY THIS SIMPLE TECHNIQUE ON A HALL TABLE, A BEDHEAD OR IN A CHILD'S PLAYROOM FOR A WITTY, EYE-CATCHING EFFECT WHICH WILL CERTAINLY NOT PASS UNNOTICED.

1 Prepare the surface of the chest of drawers by sanding lightly to remove any wax or sheen.

2 Rub over with apple-green wood dye to give a subtle veil of colour. Paint the drawer handles with forest-green gouache. Add touches of black, white and brown to add depth. Leave to dry and seal with a coat of quick-drying acrylic varnish.

3 Tape the drawers securely shut. Apply glue to the pedestal, then wrap forest-green twine around the pedestal in even, parallel rows. Draw a trailing leaf design lightly on to the top of the chest with a pencil. Carefully paint glue over a small section of the design.

4 Apply the forest-green twine over the glue. Pinch the ends of the leaves to give a defined shape. Continue gluing and applying string to small sections of the design until it is complete.

5 Apply leaf-green twine in a curving pattern over the forest-green twine on the pedestal. Leave to dry thoroughly.

6 Remove the adhesive tape from the drawers. Using a craft knife, cut through the pieces of twine at the points where they prevent the drawers from opening.

MATERIALS AND EQUIPMENT YOU WILL NEED

SMALL CHEST OF DRAWERS • SANDPAPER • APPLE-GREEN WATER-BASED WOOD DYE • KITCHEN PAPER OR SOFT CLOTH • PLASTIC GLOVES •
GOUACHE PAINTS: FOREST-GREEN, LAMP-BLACK, ZINC-WHITE AND VANDYKE-BROWN • FINE PAINTBRUSH • QUICK-DRYING ACRYLIC VARNISH •
VARNISH BRUSH • ADHESIVE TAPE • PENCIL • HIGH-TACK PVA GLUE • GLUE BRUSH • GARDEN TWINE: FOREST-GREEN AND LEAF-GREEN • CRAFT KNIFE

BOTTLE CARRIER

PERFECT FOR TRANSPORTING BOTTLES IN STYLE, BE IT HOME FROM THE SUPERMARKET OR ON A SUMMER PICNIC, THIS INGENIOUS CARRIER HOLDS THE BOTTLES SECURELY IN PLACE, REGARDLESS OF HOW MANY IT CONTAINS. THE CARRIER HOLDS UP TO FOUR BOTTLES. THIS PROJECT IS AN IDEAL OPPORTUNITY TO PRACTISE SOME BASIC KNOTS. THE HANDLE IS WORKED IN TWO DIFFERENT KNOTS, BOTH SHOWN IN BASIC TECHNIQUES. THE REST OF THE BOTTLE CARRIER IS COILED AND STITCHED WITH WAXED TWINE, MAKING IT VERY STRONG.

1 For the handle, cut two 30 cm (12 in) lengths of rope and lay them side by side on a flat surface. Lay a 3 m (10 ft) length to one side of these two pieces and another 3 m (10 ft) length to the other side, matching the centres of all four lengths. Start to work a flat knot (see Basic Techniques).

2 Work another flat knot but this time in the opposite direction. The alternating knots will make an interesting pattern.

3 Continue working flat knots until the short lengths of rope are almost used up. Fold the handle in half. Work a crown sennit knot with the remaining four long lengths of rope (see Basic Techniques). ▶

MATERIALS AND EQUIPMENT YOU WILL NEED
FLAX ROPE, APPROXIMATELY 26 M (28 YD) • TAPE MEASURE • CRAFT KNIFE • BLACK WAXED TWINE • LARGE SEWING NEEDLE •
MASKING TAPE • CURVED SEWING NEEDLE • UNWAXED TWINE

4 Continue working crown sennit knots to make a handle of the required length.

5 For the basket, start coiling the remaining length of rope around the base of the handle. Sew the coil together as you work with black waxed twine and a large needle. When the coil is two or three thicknesses of rope wide, remove it from the handle.

6 Continue producing a coil, securing the rope in place with diagonal stitches that go round two thicknesses of rope at a time. When the coil is large enough to hold four bottles, square off the shape, leaving a gap at each corner, and start working up the sides. Keep the tension even and check frequently that the bottles will fit. The rope will tend to work its way inwards, so keep the rope loose and the twine tight.

7 Work up the sides and, when they are the required height, cut off the rope at an angle with a craft knife. Wrap the end in masking tape to prevent it from unravelling.

8 Push the handle down through the hole in the bottom of the carrier. Spread each rope at the end of the handle into its individual strands and sew on to the base of the carrier using a curved needle and unwaxed twine.

BLANKET DECORATION

THE SOFT, SUBTLE COLOURS AND TEXTURE OF WOOLLEN BLANKETS COMBINE BEAUTIFULLY WITH THE NATURAL TONES AND TEXTURE OF STRING AND ROPE. INSTEAD OF THROWING AWAY OLD, FRAYED BLANKETS, TRANSFORM THEM INTO COSY, STYLISH THROWS FOR YOUR LIVING ROOM.

BLANKETS WITH WORN EDGES CAN EASILY BE FRINGED OR NEATENED WITH BLANKET STITCH, USING SOFT WHITE COTTON STRING. ANOTHER STRIKING IDEA IS TO APPLIQUÉ STRANDS OF SISAL ROPE ON TO A BLANKET, ALLOWING THE STRANDS TO FALL NATURALLY.

1 For the blanket stitch border, start by machine stitching new hems at each end, if necessary, using matching thread. Turn under the hemmed ends of the blanket. Thread a bodkin or large-eyed darning needle with the cotton string and secure on the back of the blanket with a knot concealed within the first hem. Bring the needle through to the front of the fabric. Work the border in blanket stitch (see Basic Techniques), taking care to keep the tension even. Finish with a knot concealed within the hem.

2 For the appliquéd blanket, cut off the ends of the blanket and fringe the edges by gently removing some of the threads, using a needle. Carefully separate the strands of the sisal rope.

3 Place the blanket on a flat surface and lay a single strand of rope on top, allowing it to fall naturally in a smooth, curving design. Hold the rope in position with safety pins then secure with small hand stitches, using a natural-coloured thread. Appliqué two more strands of rope in the same way.

MATERIALS AND EQUIPMENT YOU WILL NEED
2 WOOLLEN BLANKETS • SEWING MACHINE (OPTIONAL) • MATCHING MACHINE SEWING THREAD (OPTIONAL) • BODKIN OR LARGE-EYED DARNING NEEDLE • SOFT WHITE COTTON STRING • SEWING NEEDLE • ROUGH-TEXTURED SISAL ROPE • SAFETY PINS • NATURAL-COLOURED SEWING THREAD

SEWING BASKET

THE BASIC COILING AND STITCHING TECHNIQUE USED TO MAKE THIS BASKET CAN BE ADAPTED TO PRODUCE A WHOLE RANGE OF BASKETS TO SUIT A VARIETY OF APPLICATIONS. YOU CAN VARY THE WEIGHT OF STRING OR ROPE USED, DEPENDING ON THE SIZE OF BASKET YOU WISH TO MAKE. THICK ROPE, LIKE THE EIGHT-PLAIT ROPE USED IN THIS PROJECT, GIVES PLEASINGLY QUICK RESULTS; ALTERNATIVELY, YOU CAN USE THIN STRING OR TWINE TO MAKE CHARMING MINIATURE BASKETS FOR HOLDING DRESSING TABLE REQUISITES OR JEWELLERY.

1 To start the base, coil the end of the rope tightly in your hands.

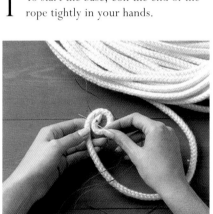

2 Thread a large needle with the red waxed twine and begin to sew the coil together as you work.

3 Continue producing a coil to form the base of the basket, securing the rope in place with random diagonal stitches that go round two thicknesses of rope at a time. The red twine stitches make an effective contrast pattern against the white rope.

4 When the base is of the required size, start working up the sides. Keep the tension even throughout. The rope will tend to work its way inwards, so keep the rope loose and the twine tight. When the sides are the required height, cut off the rope at an angle with a craft knife. Wrap the cut end in masking tape to prevent it from unravelling.

▶

MATERIALS AND EQUIPMENT YOU WILL NEED

WHITE POLYESTER EIGHT-PLAIT ROPE, APPROXIMATELY 20 M (22 YD) • LARGE NEEDLE • RED WAXED TWINE • CRAFT KNIFE • MASKING TAPE •
WHITE COTTON FABRIC • SCISSORS • DRESSMAKER'S PINS • SEWING NEEDLE • WHITE SEWING THREAD

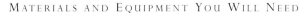

5 For the handle, fold a short length of rope in half. Bind the red twine around the loop and whip to secure (see Basic Techniques).

7 Stitch the coil together with the red twine in the same way as the base and sides of the basket.

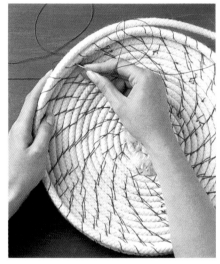

9 Make the lid slightly larger than the base so that it will fit comfortably on top, then work the sides and finish in the same way as for the base.

6 For the lid, start coiling the end of another piece of rope around the base of the whipped handle.

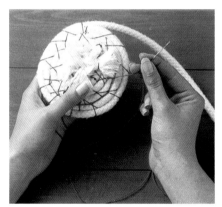

8 Stitch the loose ends of the handle securely in place on the underside of the lid.

10 Cut a circle of fabric to fit inside the basket plus a 2 cm (¾ in) seam allowance. Turn under the raw edge twice and pin around the inside rim of the basket, pleating the excess into neat folds. Stitch neatly in place. You can line the lid in the same way if required.

KNOTTED DECKCHAIR COVER

T HE COMPLEX APPEARANCE OF THIS WONDERFULLY TACTILE DECKCHAIR COVER BELIES THE SIMPLICITY OF THE KNOTTING INVOLVED. ONLY THE MOST ELEMENTARY KNOTS ARE USED, AND THE DESIGN IS WORKED IN CHUNKY SASH CORD TO PRODUCE GRATIFYINGLY SPEEDY RESULTS. THE DESIGN IS SHOWN HERE IN DETAIL ON A CHILD'S DECKCHAIR, BUT THE INSTRUCTIONS APPLY EQUALLY TO AN ADULT SIZE DECKCHAIR. AS WELL AS BEING STRONG AND HARDWEARING, THE JUTE COVER IS ALSO EXTREMELY COMFORTABLE TO SIT ON.

1 Remove the existing cover from the deckchair by taking out the staples with pliers and a screwdriver. Stand the deckchair frame on a flat surface so that the bottom seat rail is at the top and at a comfortable working height. Measure the existing cover and cut lengths of the sash cord eight times this length using a craft knife.

2 Fold each length of cord in half. Attach cords from left to right along the bottom rail using lark's head knots (see Basic Techniques). Leave the tails of the knots hanging down. Make sure that the rail is completely covered and that the total number of hanging tails is divisible by four.

3 Starting from the left-hand side of the rail, work flat knots (see Basic Techniques) on groups of four hanging tails all the way across to the right-hand side. Repeat to form a second row of flat knots, again working from left to right.

▶

MATERIALS AND EQUIPMENT YOU WILL NEED
DECKCHAIR • PLIERS • SCREWDRIVER • UNWAXED JUTE SASH CORD • CRAFT KNIFE

4 Leaving aside the first two cords, work flat knots on groups of four cords from the left to the right. Leave aside the last two cords.

6 Pass the loose end of this cord beneath the second cord and through the loop. Pull to secure, forming a chained half-hitch knot.

8 Repeat steps 3–7 until the cover is of the required length to fit the deckchair.

5 Holding the second cord from the left taut, bring the first cord out to the left to form a loop which passes over the second cord, as shown.

7 Make another chained half-hitch knot directly below the first, but this time passing the first cord under rather than over the second cord. Repeat steps 5–7, this time using the two loose cords on the right-hand side.

9 Tie the tails securely to the top rail of the deckchair using simple knots. Cover the top rail completely by wrapping two out of each group of four cords twice around the rail before tying off.

PAINTED WALL DECORATION

THE POSSIBILITIES AFFORDED BY THIS UNUSUAL BUT REFRESHINGLY SIMPLE DECORATIVE TECHNIQUE ARE LIMITED ONLY BY YOUR IMAGINATION AND THE TIME AVAILABLE. VERY DETAILED OR COMPLEX DESIGNS CAN BE WORKED ON LARGE AREAS, USING VARIED WEIGHTS OF CORD OR ROPE TO PROVIDE EXTRA TEXTURAL INTEREST. ALTERNATIVELY, YOU COULD RUN A SIMPLE CORD OR ROPE BORDER IN AN UNDULATING WAVE DESIGN AROUND THE TOP OF A BATHROOM WALL TO REINFORCE A NAUTICAL OR SEASIDE DECOR.

1 On the left-hand side of a large piece of tracing paper, draw half of the design. Join two pieces of tracing paper together with masking tape if necessary. Use a ruler and set square to ensure that the straight lines and angles are accurate. Fold the paper in half and trace over the design on to the right-hand side of the paper. Open the paper out and fold in half the other way to check the design is symmetrical.

2 Turn the tracing over and rub over the back of the design using the side of the pencil point. Stick the back of the tracing to the wall you wish to decorate, with masking tape. Using a sharp pencil so that you can easily see your progress, draw firmly over the lines of the design. This will transfer it to the wall. Remove the tracing paper.

3 Apply glue along the pencil lines on the wall, working in small sections. Stick on the piping cord, wrapping the raw ends with adhesive tape to prevent them from unravelling.

4 When the glue is completely dry, paint over the whole design in the same colour as the wall, dabbing around the string and into the corners to ensure a good coverage. Leave to dry, then touch up any areas where the string still shows through.

MATERIALS AND EQUIPMENT YOU WILL NEED

TRACING PAPER • SOFT PENCIL • LOW-TACK MASKING TAPE • RULER • SET SQUARE • SHARP COLOURED PENCIL • HIGH-TACK PVA GLUE • GLUE BRUSH • PIPING CORD • ADHESIVE TAPE • EMULSION PAINT • DECORATOR'S PAINTBRUSH

ROPE-WRAPPED CHAIR

WRAPPED IN SISAL ROPE, A BATTERED OLD JUNK SHOP CHAIR NOT ONLY ACQUIRES A NEW LEASE OF LIFE AS A BEAUTIFUL PIECE OF FURNITURE BUT BECOMES AN OBJECT OF ALMOST SCULPTURAL IMPACT. IT DOESN'T MATTER HOW DAMAGED THE SURFACE OF THE CHAIR IS AS IT WILL BE COMPLETELY COVERED BY THE ROPE, BUT TRY TO FIND ONE THAT HAS A PLEASING BASIC SHAPE. OLD-FASHIONED WOODEN KITCHEN CHAIRS OR WINDSOR CHAIRS WOULD BE VERY SUITABLE. COMPLETE THE EFFECT WITH A PLAIN CALICO CUSHION.

1 Prepare the chair by cleaning and sanding it to remove any paint or varnish that will prevent the glue from adhering. Fill any major damage with wood filler to provide a smooth, even surface. Allow to dry thoroughly, then sand off any excess.

2 Wrap the rope around the back rail of the chair, gluing it securely in place. Glue lengths of rope across the back of the seat of the chair and cut them off at the back uprights using a craft knife and cutting mat. Glue lengths of rope across the front of the seat, following the curve carefully.

3 Cut a few short lengths of rope, each one slightly shorter than the next. Glue the short lengths of rope in place to form a triangle on the upright at each side of the back rail (see step 7).

MATERIALS AND EQUIPMENT YOU WILL NEED

NICELY SHAPED WOODEN CHAIR • SANDPAPER • WOOD FILLER • SISAL ROPE • HIGH-TACK PVA GLUE • GLUE SPREADER • CRAFT KNIFE • CUTTING MAT • LARGE CLIPS

4 Wrap the brace between the legs of the chair, adding triangles of rope at the intersections, as before. Begin to wrap the arm rail of the chair, working from the seat upwards. Use large clips to hold the rope in place while the glue dries.

5 Add more rope across the front of the seat until the edges are aligned with the rope wrapping the arm rail.

6 Holding the rope securely in place with clips while the glue dries, carefully cut off the excess rope.

7 Glue another length of rope across the back of the seat, just in front of the uprights.

8 Wrap the legs, making sure that all the intersections have a triangle of short lengths of rope, as before.

9 Wrap and glue rope around the top rail of the chair. Bring the rope down the arm rail and glue in place. Take care that the rope is exactly in line with the arm of the chair.

10 Wrap and glue an additional length of rope around the front of each arm to conceal any raw edges.

12 Glue a length of rope across the centre of the seat from the back to the front, holding the end with a clip. Trim to length. Add more lengths of rope either side of this first length to completely cover the seat.

11 Holding the end securely in a clip, glue rope diagonally over the join between the top rail and each back upright. Overwrap any other joins that need to be either concealed or embellished.

FRINGED SHELF EDGING

THE SIMPLEST AND MOST INEXPENSIVE OF SHELVES ASSUMES DESIGNER STATUS WHEN ADORNED WITH A FRIVOLOUS SKIRT OF RAFFIA. YOU CAN ADAPT THE TECHNIQUE TO SUIT DEEPER SHELVING, EITHER BY PLAITING WITH MORE STRANDS OF RAFFIA OR BY USING THICK ROPE INSTEAD. IF YOU ARE USING ROPE, FRAY THE ENDS TO PRODUCE THE FRINGED EFFECT. YOU CAN TRIM THE ENDS OR LEAVE THEM IRREGULAR FOR A NATURAL LOOK.

1 Bunch together 60 strands of raffia about one and a half times as long as the shelf to be edged. Attach one end to a door handle or nail using an elastic band.

3 To produce a flat braid, keep your thumbs uppermost, as turning your thumbs towards the centre would produce a round cord.

5 Pull the loose ends through the loop to form a lark's head knot (see Basic Techniques). Add bunches of raffia along the whole length of the plait in the same way. Trim the ends to make an even fringe if required.

2 Divide the raffia into three groups of 20 strands and begin to plait evenly.

4 Cut some shorter pieces of raffia and group them in bunches of ten. Fold the first group of ten in half to form a loop. Push this loop through one of the loops in the plait.

6 Finally, attach the shelf edging to the shelf using drawing pins or double-sided tape.

MATERIALS AND EQUIPMENT YOU WILL NEED
RAFFIA • SHELF • LARGE ELASTIC BAND • SCISSORS • DRAWING PINS OR DOUBLE-SIDED TAPE

FOOD COVER

SHOP-BOUGHT FOOD COVERS ARE ALL TOO OFTEN RATHER GARISH STRUCTURES OF BRIGHTLY COLOURED PLASTIC SUPPORTING A LAYER OF UNATTRACTIVE NYLON MESH. IN THIS VERY DIFFERENT COVER, FABRIC STIFFENER TURNS ORDINARY WHITE COTTON STRING INTO A SCULPTURAL MATERIAL THAT WILL RETAIN THE MOST UNEXPECTED SHAPES INDEFINITELY. SHORT LENGTHS OF JUTE TWINE, SIMPLY KNOTTED AND FRAYED, ADD A PRETTY DECORATION OF WISPY BUTTERFLIES TO COMPLETE THIS VERY UNUSUAL KITCHEN ACCESSORY.

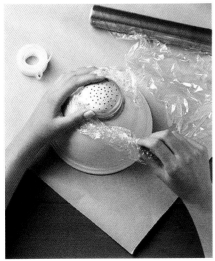

1 Place the flour sifter lid or other small, dome-shaped item on the base of an upturned plastic bowl. Pad out the shape with clear plastic wrap to make the mould for the food cover and secure with adhesive tape. Cover the whole mould in plastic wrap to produce a smooth surface.

2 Smear the mould with petroleum jelly and cover with another layer of plastic wrap.

3 Pour the fabric stiffener into a large bowl. Cut a generous length of string. Wearing plastic gloves, place the string into the bowl and squeeze the liquid into the string until the string is saturated with fabric stiffener. ▶

MATERIALS AND EQUIPMENT YOU WILL NEED

LID OF FLOUR SIFTER OR SIMILAR SMALL, DOME-SHAPED ITEM • PLASTIC BOWL • CLEAR PLASTIC WRAP •ADHESIVE TAPE • PETROLEUM JELLY • FABRIC STIFFENER • LARGE BOWL • WHITE COTTON STRING • SCISSORS • PLASTIC GLOVES • JUTE TWINE • HIGH-TACK PVA GLUE • GLUE SPREADER

4 Lay lengths of string in evenly spaced parallel lines over the mould, starting in the centre and working down each side. Cut off each length, leaving some overhanging the edge. The weight of these long ends will help form a neat finished shape. Continue until the mould is covered.

6 Wrap a length of saturated string three times around the base of the mould to form a firm rim. Twist two short lengths of saturated string together to make a handle. Form into a circle and attach to the top of the structure, tucking the ends neatly into the layers of string. Leave to dry overnight.

8 Twist a short length of jute twine around the handle and glue in place with high-tack PVA glue, neatly tucking in the raw ends.

5 Again starting in the centre, lay a second layer of string lengths on top of the first, in the opposite direction. Space and trim this layer as before.

7 When completely dry, gently twist the food cover to release the surface tension and remove from the mould.

9 Tie short lengths of jute twine in simple knots randomly over the surface of the food cover. Fray the ends to make decorative "butterflies".

NATURAL CURTAIN

HUNG WITH NATURAL KEEPSAKES COLLECTED DURING EXPEDITIONS TO THE SEASHORE AND COUNTRYSIDE, THIS SIMPLE STRANDED CURTAIN IS A KIND OF "LIVING SCRAPBOOK". NEW OBJECTS CAN BE ADDED AS THEY ARE ACQUIRED, AND THE SLIGHTLY ROUGH TEXTURE OF THE JUTE TWINE HOLDS EACH OBJECT PERFECTLY IN PLACE. A FALLEN BRANCH MAKES THE IDEAL SUPPORT. AMBER, STRAY FEATHERS, EVEN HUMBLE TWIGS AND BOTTLE TOPS ALL ASSUME TALISMANIC IMPORTANCE WHEN DISPLAYED WITH SUCH ADMIRABLE RESTRAINT.

1 Cut the branch to fit the width of your window and secure at a comfortable working height by hanging with twine. Cut lengths of jute twine twice the required height of the curtain. Fold each length of twine in half and pass the folded end over the branch from front to back.

2 Pass the ends of each length of twine through the loop and pull tight, forming a lark's head knot (see Basic Techniques). Attach the lengths of twine along the branch in this way at equal intervals.

3 Hold the beads and various found objects up against the lengths of twine to begin planning your design. Drill a hole in the objects if required.

▶

MATERIALS AND EQUIPMENT YOU WILL NEED

BRANCH • HAIRY JUTE TWINE • SCISSORS • SELECTION OF FOUND OBJECTS: LEAVES, BEADS, SHELLS, CRUSHED BOTTLE TOPS, TWIGS, SEMI-PRECIOUS STONES, ETC. • DRILL (OPTIONAL) • INSTANT-BONDING GLUE

4 Apply a few drops of instant-bonding glue to the end of each piece of twine and allow to dry, to make threading easier.

6 Thread a second object on to the next piece of twine, but at a slightly different height.

8 Vary the planes in which the objects lie by making two holes in suitable objects, such as bottle tops. Thread the twine through one of the holes from the back to the front. Now thread the twine back through the other hole so that the bottle top or other object lies flat against the twine.

5 Thread one of the collection of objects on to the twine and tie a knot below it to hold it in place.

7 Vary the design by attaching some items with a reverse lark's head knot. Fold the twine to form a loop at the point at which you want to attach the object. Push the loop through the hole in the object and pass the remaining length of twine through the loop.

9 Take care to pull the twine very gently through fragile objects such as dried leaves or feathers.

NAUTICAL LIGHT PULL

THIS OUTSIZE LIGHT PULL REPLACES THE WHITE NYLON LIGHT PULLS, WHICH CAN SO EASILY BECOME GRUBBY, FOUND IN SO MANY HOMES. CORD TIED WITH A FEW SIMPLE KNOTS GIVES IT A JAUNTY NAUTICAL APPEARANCE THAT YOU CAN EXTEND AS A THEME FOR DECORATING THE WHOLE BATHROOM. THE CHUNKY KNOTS AND BEADS GIVE A PLEASING CONTRAST OF TEXTURE EVERY TIME YOU SWITCH THE LIGHT ON OR OFF. YOU COULD ALSO MAKE A BLIND PULL IN THE SAME WAY, USING NATURAL-COLOURED CORD AND WOODEN BEADS.

1 Fold the cord in half and pinch together to mark the centre point.

2 Use one half of the cord to form three blanket stitches around the other half of the cord, working along from the centre (see Basic Techniques).

3 Glue the halves of the cord together along their length, leaving the last 5 cm (2 in) free. Hold them together with clips while the glue dries.

4 Glue the red beads between the loops as decoration. Alternatively, stitch the beads in place with matching sewing thread.

To fit the light pull, unscrew and remove the existing light pull, leaving the part attached to the ceiling still in place. Bring the two ends of the sash cord up around the part of the light pull that is attached to the ceiling. Using matching or contrasting twine, whip securely in place around the remaining part of the light pull, concealing it within the whipping (see Basic Techniques).

MATERIALS AND EQUIPMENT YOU WILL NEED
RED-AND-WHITE SASH CORD, 2.10 M (7 FT) LONG • HIGH-TACK PVA GLUE • GLUE SPREADER • LARGE CLIPS • RED BEADS •
SEWING NEEDLE AND MATCHING THREAD (OPTIONAL) • MATCHING OR CONTRASTING TWINE

STRING-APPLIQUÉD CURTAINS

ORDINARY WHITE COTTON STRING IS EXCELLENT FOR LARGE-SCALE FURNISHING PROJECTS SUCH AS THESE FULL-LENGTH CURTAINS. THE APPEALING, CHILD-LIKE DESIGN OF LARGE DAISY FLOWERS IS APPLIQUÉD DIRECTLY ON TO THE PLAIN BACKGROUND FABRIC. FOR A CHILD'S ROOM YOU COULD STITCH THE WHITE FLOWERS ON TO A BRIGHT-COLOURED FABRIC. COMPLETE THE WINDOW DECORATION WITH THESE SPLENDID TASSELLED CURTAIN POLE FINIALS — FEW PEOPLE WILL REALIZE THAT THEY ARE, IN FACT, MADE FROM TWO OLD-FASHIONED FLOOR MOPS!

1 Decide on the size of the finished curtains. Add 5 cm (2 in) to the width and 9 cm (3½ in) to the length and cut the curtains from the linen or linen-look fabric. Fold in 1 cm (½ in) along the long sides of the fabric and press. Fold over again 1.5 cm (⅝ in). Pin, tack and stitch the hems, then press.

2 Measure the width of the curtains and decide how many tabs are needed, assuming that the tabs will be 7 cm (2¾ in) wide with 9 cm (3½ in) gaps between them. Multiply the number of tabs by 24 cm (9½ in); cut a strip of fabric to this length and 17 cm (6½ in) wide. Fold the strip of fabric in half lengthways. Pin, tack and stitch along the long edge with right sides together, leaving a 1.5 cm (½ in) seam allowance.

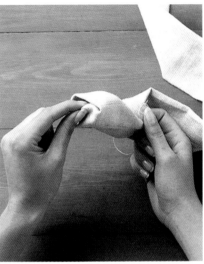

3 Press the seams open. Turn the tubes the right way out and press flat with the seam positioned centrally on one side of the tube. Cut the strip into 24 cm (9½ in) lengths. Tuck a foldover of 1 cm (½ in) at each end inside the tab. Pin, tack and stitch in place. ▶

MATERIALS AND EQUIPMENT YOU WILL NEED

LINEN OR LINEN-LOOK FABRIC • TAPE MEASURE • SCISSORS • IRON • DRESSMAKER'S PINS • SEWING NEEDLE • TACKING THREAD • MATCHING THREAD • SEWING MACHINE (OPTIONAL) • DRESSMAKER'S PENCIL • WHITE COTTON STRING • WHITE SEWING THREAD • 2 MOP HEADS • SCRAP PAPER • MASKING TAPE • COPPER PAINT • PAINTBRUSH • 2 METAL BRACKETS TO FIT DIAMETER OF POLE • COPPER POLE TO FIT THE WINDOW • GLUE GUN AND GLUE STICKS

4 Fold in 1 cm (½ in) along the top edge of the curtains and press. Fold over another 3 cm (1¼ in). Pin, tack and stitch the hems. Fold the tabs in half and pin on to the curtains, leaving 9 cm (3½ in) gaps between them. Line up the bottom of the tabs with the bottom of the hem. Tack and stitch in place. Fold in 1 cm (½ in) along the bottom of the curtains and then another 4 cm (1½ in). Pin, tack and stitch the bottom hems.

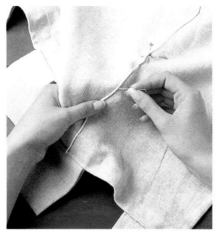

6 Tuck the end of the white cotton string over the top of the curtain. Stitch securely in place with a needle and white thread. Pin the string along the marked line, approximately 30 cm (12 in) at a time or up to a floral motif marker. Hand stitch in place using tiny slip stitches.

8 Cover the string on the mop heads with scrap paper to protect it. Stick a piece of masking tape around the metal top. Paint the wooden part with copper paint and leave to dry.

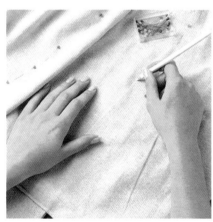

5 Lay the curtains right side up on a flat surface. Measure lines from the top to the bottom of the curtains approximately 45 cm (18 in) apart. Mark with pins, then draw the lines with a dressmaker's pencil. Decide on the positions of the floral motifs, approximately 60 cm (23½ in) apart, and mark with pins.

7 To sew a floral motif, loop the string to form a petal shape and pin in place. Stitch the petal to the fabric. Repeat until the flower has six petals. Continue stitching the string down the marked pencil line to the bottom of the curtain. When the string appliqué is complete, carefully press the curtains.

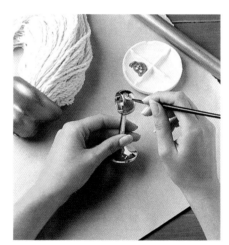

9 Paint the metal brackets with copper paint. When dry, thread the curtain tabs on to the copper pole and thread a bracket on to each end. Glue the mop head finials on to each end of the pole using a glue gun. (The hot-melt glue can be snapped off when the curtains need laundering and reapplied when they are re-hung.) Attach the brackets to the wall above the window.

GREETINGS CARD

INEXPENSIVE SCRAPS OF PAPER TAKE ON A SOPHISTICATED AIR WHEN DELICATELY BOUND TOGETHER BY A LENGTH OF JUTE STRING TO FORM A UNIQUE HANDMADE CARD. STRANDS PULLED FROM A PIECE OF PLASTERER'S SCRIM WILL GIVE YOU LENGTHS OF JUTE OF SUITABLE FINENESS. THE SIMPLE CUT-OUT OAK LEAF MOTIF PROVIDES A PERFECTLY MATCHED GIFT TAG. IF YOU SCENT THE OIL USED TO MAKE THE PAPER TRANSLUCENT, THIS WILL GIVE THE CARD A REALLY SPECIAL EXTRA-SENSORY DIMENSION.

1 Scent some olive oil with a little essential oil, if desired. Working on a protected surface, use kitchen paper to rub the olive oil over a sheet of calligraphy paper until it becomes translucent. Leave to dry.

2 Cut a piece of green sugar paper to form the front of the card. Draw an oak leaf shape approximately one-third of the way down from the top.

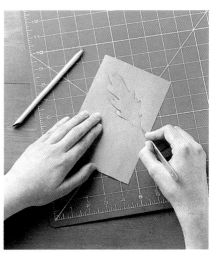

3 Cut out the leaf shape with a craft knife on a cutting mat. Put the leaf shape to one side.

▶

MATERIALS AND EQUIPMENT YOU WILL NEED

OLIVE OIL • ESSENTIAL OIL (OPTIONAL) • KITCHEN PAPER • CALLIGRAPHY PAPER • GREEN SUGAR PAPER • SCISSORS • PENCIL • CRAFT KNIFE • CUTTING MAT • PAPER GLUE • WATERCOLOUR PAPER • METAL RULER • HIGH-TACK PVA GLUE • BODKIN • FINE JUTE TWINE OR PLASTERER'S JUTE SCRIM

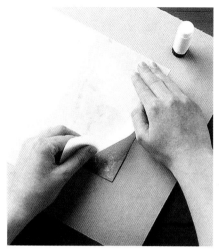

4 Glue the oiled paper on top of the sugar paper. The oil will cause uneven sticking, which gives the finished card a pleasingly mottled appearance. Leave until completely dry under a pile of books. Protect the books with several layers of kitchen paper to absorb any residual oil.

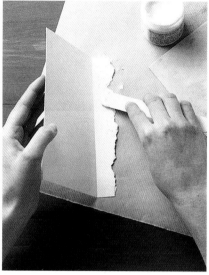

6 Cut the oiled paper to the same size as the green paper. Apply glue to the top two-thirds of the torn side of the folded watercolour paper. Glue the layered green paper and oiled paper in place to form the front of the greetings card.

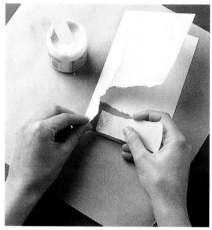

8 Cut a piece of green paper and a piece of oiled paper to the width of the greetings card, about half the height of the gap left below the oiled and green paper. Tear across the top edges. Glue the green paper to the inside of the card along the bottom and glue the oiled paper to the torn edge.

5 Score down the centre of the watercolour paper using the back of a craft knife and a metal ruler, and fold to make the greetings card. Tear away most of the paper to one side of the fold to produce a deckled edge.

7 Tear across the front of the greetings card just below where the glue ends and remove the bottom third.

9 Make holes in the front of the card with a bodkin and thread through the twine to join the upper and lower parts. Tie a simple knot at each end of the string.
    For the gift tag, make a hole in the cut-out leaf shape. Attach a length of string to the leaf using a lark's head knot (see Basic Techniques). Carefully score a central, curving vein along the leaf using the back of the craft knife.

KEY CUPBOARD

THE SECRET OF PERFECT STORAGE IS ACCESSIBILITY AND VISIBILITY, ALLOWING INSTANT RETRIEVAL OF STORED OBJECTS. REPLACING THE SOLID FRONT OF THIS WOODEN CUPBOARD WITH A SINGLE LENGTH OF THREADED TWINE MEANS THAT YOU WILL NOT BE IN ANY DOUBT AS TO THE WHEREABOUTS OF THE KEY TO THE COCKTAIL CABINET. ATTACH NAILS TO THE BACK OF THE CUPBOARD FOR HANGING THE KEYS. THE CUPBOARD WOULD ALSO BE A USEFUL PLACE TO KEEP JEWELLERY OR OTHER VALUABLES BEAUTIFULLY DISPLAYED.

1 Cut into the rebate on the back of the cupboard door using a scalpel and metal ruler. In the interests of safety and accuracy, do not attempt to cut through the entire thickness of the wood at once; instead make several shallow cuts. Remove the solid door panel.

2 Measure and note the dimensions of the rebate.

3 Cut strips of soft wood to make the four sides of a simple frame that will fit snugly into the rebate. Tape the two shorter pieces together with masking tape. Drill a row of evenly spaced 3 mm (1/8 in) holes through both pieces simultaneously.

4 Glue the four sides of the frame together with a glue gun, making sure that the holes along the top and bottom of the frame are facing each other.

5 Thread the jute twine through the holes from top to bottom in one continuous length and maintaining an even tension. Secure the twine with a simple knot at each end.

6 Glue the string screen into the rebate. Cut lengths of masking tape to cover the join.

MATERIALS AND EQUIPMENT YOU WILL NEED

SMALL WOODEN KEY CUPBOARD • SCALPEL • METAL RULER • PENCIL AND PAPER • STRIPS OF SOFT WOOD • MASKING TAPE •
DRILL AND WOOD BIT • GLUE GUN AND GLUE STICKS • JUTE TWINE

WOVEN STOOL SEAT

MANY HOMES HAVE AT LEAST ONE RUSH STOOL OR CHAIR SEAT THAT WOULD BENEFIT FROM RENOVATION BUT IS NOT WORTH THE EXPENSE OF PROFESSIONAL ATTENTION. RUSH OR SEAGRASS IS NOT ALWAYS READILY AVAILABLE TODAY, AND THE NOTION OF LEARNING WHAT SEEMS TO BE A SPECIALIST CRAFT CAN BE A LITTLE DAUNTING. INSTEAD, THIS SIMPLE WEAVING TECHNIQUE ALLOWS YOU TO USE ROPE FOR THE SEAT, TO GREAT PRACTICAL AND VISUAL EFFECT. THE LARGE, BLUNT WOODEN AWL IS A VERY USEFUL TOOL FOR THIS PROJECT.

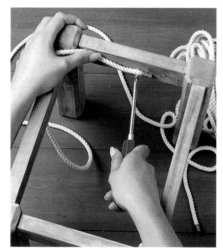

1 Divide the rope into three bundles for ease of handling. Mark each cut and bind in each place with masking tape to stop the ends fraying when you cut. Choose a screw that is long enough to go through the end of the rope and into the wood of the stool without coming out on the other side. Screw through the end of one of the rope bundles and into the centre of the first strut (strut A), on the inside of the stool.

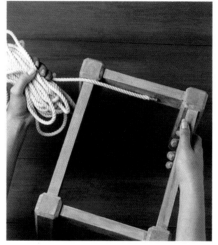

2 Pull the rope parallel with strut A and take it over the second strut (strut B).

3 Take the rope all the way around strut B and then back over strut A, as shown. Maintain an even tension on the rope as you work.

MATERIALS AND EQUIPMENT YOU WILL NEED

6 MM (¼ IN) UNBLEACHED COTTON ROPE, APPROXIMATELY 36 M (39 YD) • CRAFT KNIFE • MASKING TAPE • 2 WOOD SCREWS •
RUSH STOOL WITH SEAT REMOVED • SCREWDRIVER • LARGE NEEDLE • TWINE OR STRONG THREAD • LARGE WOODEN AWL

4 Bring the rope up through the middle of the stool and over the third strut (strut C).

6 Using twine or strong thread, stitch the end of the rope securely to the adjacent piece of rope.

8 When the short sides of the stool are complete, work the middle of the stool in a figure-of-eight, joining on more rope as necessary.

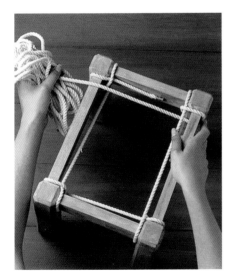

5 Continue working around the stool in this way, passing the rope over and around each consecutive strut, until you reach the end of the first bundle.

7 Wrap the end of the next bundle of rope with masking tape and stitch it in place so that it butts up to the end of the first bundle.

9 The weaving will become tighter and more difficult to work as you fill the centre. Use a large awl to create as much space as possible until no more rope can be fitted in.

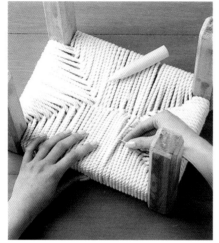

10 Finish off the loose end of the last bundle of rope by stitching it as in step 6. Tuck the end neatly inside the weaving.

11 Finally, use the awl to flatten out and neaten up any irregularities in the weaving.

NAPKIN RING

THIS DELIGHTFULLY SIMPLE EXAMPLE OF STRINGWORK IS MADE USING TWO DIFFERENT KINDS OF STRING LOOSELY TWISTED TOGETHER AND TREATED AS ONE STRAND. SOFT WHITE COTTON STRING COMBINES BEAUTIFULLY WITH THE NATURAL COLOUR AND HARSHER TEXTURE OF JUTE TWINE TO GIVE AN IRRESISTIBLY TACTILE RESULT. A SET OF MATCHING NAPKIN RINGS WOULD LOOK WONDERFULLY ELEGANT WITH PLAIN LINEN NAPKINS OR A DAMASK TABLECLOTH. THE RING IS WORKED ENTIRELY IN BLANKET STITCH.

1 Cut a length of cotton string and a length of jute twine both four times the circumference of the finished napkin ring. Twist the two loosely together.

3 Complete the circle and cut off any excess.

5 When you have completed the circle, cut off the loose ends and glue in place. Tuck in the raw ends neatly.

2 Form the two into a circle. Wrap one end around and through the circle several times to make a secure ring.

4 Using the remaining long end, work in blanket stitch around the circle (see Basic Techniques).

MATERIALS AND EQUIPMENT YOU WILL NEED
SOFT WHITE COTTON STRING • JUTE TWINE • SCISSORS • HIGH-TACK PVA GLUE • GLUE SPREADER

BEADED JUG COVER

ASSORTED BEADS SERVE AS DECORATION AND ALSO TO WEIGHT DOWN THIS JUG COVER, WHICH IS MADE IN MOMENTS FROM A SCRAP OF PLASTERER'S SCRIM. PLASTERER'S SCRIM IS AN OPEN-WEAVE FABRIC USED TO JOIN PLASTERWORK LAYERS AND IS READILY AVAILABLE FROM BUILDER'S MERCHANTS AND DIY STORES. THE COVER IS A STYLISH MODERN VERSION OF THE TRADITIONAL MILK JUG COVER AND IS REMINISCENT OF SUMMER MEALS OUTDOORS. THIS IS A LOVELY WAY TO USE A COLLECTION OF BEAUTIFUL OLD GLASS BEADS.

1 Drape the scrim over the jug to ascertain the required finished size.

2 Cut the scrim to the required length. Take care to cut between the weft (horizontal) threads as this will give a neat edge.

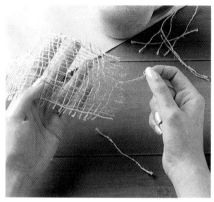

3 Gently remove a few weft threads from each cut edge by hand to produce a fringe.

4 Drip glue along the long edges of the scrim, where the warp and weft threads cross, to strengthen the edge.

5 At each corner, thread a bead on to one of the double-warp threads at the edge of the scrim, then tie the two threads in a double knot around the bead.

6 Thread beads on to the loose warp threads at each end of the scrim, tying a simple knot to secure each bead in place. Tie the knot at a different point on each thread to produce a pleasingly undulating edge.

MATERIALS AND EQUIPMENT YOU WILL NEED

JUG • SMALL PIECE OF PLASTERER'S JUTE SCRIM • SCISSORS • INSTANT-BONDING GLUE • ASSORTED GLASS BEADS

TWINE TASSEL

THIS GENEROUSLY SIZED TASSEL, WITH ITS SKIRT OF GREEN GARDEN TWINE, WOULD MAKE AN IMPOSING ADDITION TO A CURTAIN TIE-BACK, OR PROVIDE SPLENDOUR AS A TRADITIONAL KEY TASSEL. WORKED OVER A CURTAIN POLE FINIAL, THE TASSEL USES THE SIMPLEST OF PASSEMENTERIE TECHNIQUES TO STUNNING EFFECT. THE STRIPED CORD IS MADE USING TWO DIFFERENT COLOURS OF TWINE, WHICH ARE TWISTED TIGHTLY TOGETHER IN THE CHUCK OF A HAND DRILL FOR A REALLY PROFESSIONAL EFFECT.

1 To make the cord, wind the brown twine 12 times around two immobile objects 1.2 m (4 ft) apart. Wind the thinner, green twine approximately 40 times around the same two objects until it is the same thickness as the bundle of brown twine. Knot the two colours together. Secure a cup hook in the chuck of a hand drill. Loop the twines over the cup hook at one end and over a clamp or door handle at the other.

2 Turn the drill handle clockwise to twist the twine until it is so tightly spun that it is about to kink.

3 Without loosening the tension of the twisted twines, release the end that is attached to the clamp or door handle, and carefully loop it round the clamp and attach it to the cup hook, alongside the first end.

▶

MATERIALS AND EQUIPMENT YOU WILL NEED

THICK BROWN AND FINE GREEN GARDEN TWINE • SCISSORS • CUP HOOK • HAND DRILL • CLAMP (OPTIONAL) • DRILL WITH WOOD BIT • CURTAIN POLE FINIAL • THICK KNITTING NEEDLE • INSTANT-BONDING GLUE • GLUE SPREADER • MOUNTING BOARD OR WOOD, 20 x 28 CM (8 x 11 IN)

4 Turn the drill handle anti-clockwise to twist the two colours together, producing a tight cord. Bind both ends of the cord tightly to prevent them from unravelling.

6 Wind green twine 50 times around the 28 cm (11 in) length of the piece of mounting board or wood. Tie the loose ends together. Pass a short piece of twine through one end of the loop and tie off firmly. Remove the tied loop from the board. Repeat to make a total of ten loops.

8 Apply glue liberally to the top of the skirt. Remove the knitting needle from the finial, then thread the cord through the hole in the finial and pull it up so that the top of the skirt sits inside the finial. Cut through the looped bottom end of the skirt. Finally trim the tassel to an even length.

5 Drill a 1 cm (1/2 in) hole through the finial from top to bottom. Insert a thick knitting needle through the hole and apply glue liberally to the top half of the finial. Wind brown twine around the finial over the glue, starting from the top. Apply more glue and continue winding until the finial is completely covered with twine. Rotate the finial on the knitting needle to avoid overhandling so that the work remains clean.

7 Using the short piece of twine, tie each loop on to the end of the twisted cord, spacing them evenly to form the skirt of the tassel.

ACKNOWLEDGEMENTS

String and rope are widely available internationally in chandler's, hardware shops, craft shops, department stores, garden-supply stores and garden centres.

The publishers would like to thank the following craftspeople for making projects in this book: Emma Hardy for the gilded string vase, cord-trimmed cushion covers, wrapped candelabra, painted wall decoration and string-appliquéd curtain; Penny Boylan for the string-trimmed bag; Tessa Brown for the bottle carrier, sewing basket and the woven stool seat; and Anna Crutchley for the tassel.

They would also like to thank those people who kindly lent items for the gallery: Knots and Pots, Tallowater, Braddock, Lostwithiel, Cornwall PL22 0RH (01208 872271) for the dice cup and bellrope; Marjorie Self (c/o the Publishers) for the appliquéd cowboy; Paperchase, Tottenham Court Road, London, for the twine-wrapped candlestick; Lakeland Plastics, Alexandra Buildings, Windermere, Cumbria LA23 1BQ for the string bag and the wine cooler; V.V. Rouleaux, 10 Symons Street, London SW3 2TJ (0171 730 4413) for the tassels; The India Shop, 5 Hilliers Yard, Marlborough, Wiltshire SN8 1NB (01672 515585 for mail-order details and branches) for the child's hanging chair, and the Conran Shop, Fulham Road, London SW3 6RD (0171 589 7401) for the turned lanyard.

The following shops kindly supplied items for this book and may be useful sources of a range of additional items: The Bead Shop, 43 Neal Street, Covent Garden, London WC2H 7PJ (0171 240 0931); Berol (products available from arts and crafts stores, and stationers), suppliers of pencils used throughout; Bostik (0116 251 0015 for stockists), suppliers of instant-bonding glue, as well as glue guns and glue sticks; Brats, 281 King's Road, London SW3 5EW (0171 351 7674), suppliers of "Mediterranean palette" colours used; Copperstones, 105 High Street, Marlborough, Wiltshire SN8 1LT (01672 515074), suppliers of the tumblers; Country Gardens (01635 873700), suppliers of the child's deckchair; Crucial Trading (0171 221 9000 for stockists), suppliers of natural flooring; The Dollshouse Draper, Lightcliffe, Halifax, Yorkshire HX3 8RN (01422 201275 for mail-order details), suppliers of silk ribbons; The English Stamp Company, Sunnydown, Worth Matravers, Dorset BH19 3JP (01929 439117 for stockists and mail-order details), suppliers of stamping paints and applicators; The Faerie Shop, 22 Hughenden Yard, Marlborough, Wiltshire SN8 1LT (01672 515995), suppliers of additional beads; Liberon (01797 367555 for stockists), suppliers of water-based wood dye used on the twine-decorated chest of drawers; 3M Adhesives (available from arts and crafts stores, and stationers), suppliers of spray adhesive; The Natural Fabric Company, Wessex Place, 127 High Street, Hungerford, Wiltshire RG17 0DL (01488 684002), stockists of a diverse range of high-quality natural fabrics; Paint Magic, 116 Sheen Road, Richmond, Surrey SW9 1UR (0181 940 5503), suppliers of special-effect paints; Panduro (mail-order in the UK, outlets in Scandinavia, 0181 847 6161 for catalogues), suppliers of the fabric stiffener; Specialist Crafts Ltd, PO Box 247, Leicester LE1 9QS (0116 251 0405 for mail-order details), suppliers of lampshade stiffener and stockists of a huge range of craft supplies; Eliza Tinsley, supplier of rope for the wrapped chair; The White Company (0171 385 7988 for mail-order details), suppliers of elegant and useful textiles. Thanks to Faber & Faber for supplying a reference copy of *The Ashley Book of Knots*.

AUTHOR'S ACKNOWLEDGEMENTS

Special thanks to Peter Williams for his elegant photography and to Joanna Lorenz for giving me the opportunity to write this book. Thanks to all those who contributed to this book, whether by loaning items for photography or by making designs. Finally, thanks to Andrew and Daisy for supporting me during the production of this book.

INDEX

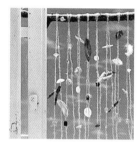